*To Your Success!*

*Frances Marx*

# How to Journal Your Way
# to Personal Success

*A Guided Tour on the Journey to Self-Discovery*

*By Frances Marx*

Published by
JFM Integrity

Published by:
JFM Integrity
6515 Tarawa Dr.
Sarasota, Fl. 34241 USA
yoursuccessadvocate@gmail.com

Author: Frances Marx
Graphic Designer: Frances Marx
Editor: JFM Integrity Editorial Staff
Second U.S. Edition Year 2014
How to Journal Your Way to Personal Success
Summary:  **A Guided Tour on the Journey to
Self-Discovery**
13 digit ISBN# 978-0-9916516-0-3

1.      How to, Self-Help, Personal Development, Success,
        Motivational, Journal

For current information about releases by Frances Marx,
Email: yoursuccessadvocate@gmail.com
Printed in the United States of America
2014

# TABLE OF CONTENTS

## PART 1 – JOURNALING

## PART 2 – SELF-DISCOVERY

## PART 3 – THOUGHTS AND CHALLENGES

## PART 4 – APPENDIX

# Part 1

# Journaling

# *Preface*

At each stage of our lives we ask ourselves this question: Who am I and where am I going? We may not use those words exactly, but we often wonder about our purpose in life and how we will achieve it. I believe that all of us have the answers within ourselves. Socrates, the ancient Greek philosopher, believed that we could find the answers within ourselves if we were asked the right questions to help us think deeply about who we really are and what we really want.

I have written this book as my humble attempt to replicate the Socratic philosophy by asking you, the readers, questions which will guide you to find your true answers to life's questions for yourself. It is my hope that you will invest the time needed to find your true selves. Because it is by making this investment into yourself that you will learn to accept and love yourself with all your strengths and weaknesses. You will also be better able to determine your interests, strengths, and life patterns, and by doing so you will be equipped to seek and find fulfillment in your life and career choices.

I have often thought how sad it is that so few people stop to think about their strengths and interests and match them to a career choice. Henry David Thoreau, famous American author, poet, and philosopher, summed it up best when he said, "Most men lead lives of quiet desperation and go to the grave with the song still in them." I challenge you to sing the song that is within you. Take the time to find your true self and use that knowledge to pursue your true passion, career, and life goals.

In writing <u>How to Journal Your Way to Personal Success: A Guided Tour on the Journey to Self-Discovery,</u> my hope is that people will use it as a tool by which they can:

- Recognize personal achievements and strengths
- Gain a sense of focus
- Gain a new understanding of themselves
- Realize their dreams and visions for the future
- Be true to themselves

Welcome and congratulations for your choice to embark on a journey of self-discovery!

# Introduction

If you want something different, you must do something different. Not sure where to start and what to do? Are you tired of seeing others succeed while you settle for mediocrity? Are you tired of believing that mediocrity is the best you can do? Are you already on the right track toward self-fulfillment, and want to fine tune your journey?

In your hands, you are holding a powerful tool. How you choose to use this tool will determine its effectiveness.

*"The secret of getting ahead, is getting started"*
*Mark Twain*

Each day make a commitment to look for, remember, and write down something good you have done or an obstacle you have overcome on that day. If you miss a day or two, don't stop, just start again. Ultimately, to make the most of this tool, you must make a habit of looking for the good in yourself and using that information for your benefit.

In our companion book, My Success Journal: Writing with a Purpose, available at www.Amazon.com each page has a quote that was carefully chosen and intended to be a word of encouragement to you. If you would like to receive these quotes on a regular basis via email, please contact me at yoursuccessadvocate@gmail.com

# *What Makes You So Special?*

What makes you so special?! At every stage of your life someone in your future will want to know why you are special.

A college, university, or trade school will want to know why they should choose you for acceptance to their school over someone else. Those who give away scholarship money will want to know the same. An employer will want to know what you have to offer him and how you can enhance his company, since he is offering a salary and possibly benefits to you. If you go into the military, you will probably prefer the job most suited to you.

If you want to get married, knowing yourself will help you to choose the best mate to complement you – he/she will be strong in areas where you are weak and you will be strong where he/she is weak. This combination makes a great team. If you can explain to yourself or others, what makes you so special, you will become confident and comfortable with yourself. As a result, you will find favor in your pursuits.

There are many components of success, starting with, "To thine own self be true." (William Shakespeare). How do we find ourselves and know who we really are? How do we find our own voice? Most of our beliefs about ourselves come from the reflections that others have shared with us.

If those we love or those significant people in our lives see us as being valuable, we believe we are. If we perceive that they don't care about us, we feel worthless. But are we - really? The answer is a resounding NO! Each of us was created for a specific purpose that only we can achieve. No one else is exactly like us. No one speaks like us, thinks like us, looks like us, has our personality, and has the gifts we have. We are each unique.

How do we realize that uniqueness? We need to examine ourselves. What makes us feel accomplished? What can we do with ease? What makes us happy?

If you don't know the answers to any of these questions, take some time to be quiet and just think about it. If you allow yourself to think freely, you will find the answers. If you build limiting barriers around your thoughts, such as, "I could never do that", "I am not capable", "My life circumstances are such that anything different is impossible", or "Others limit me", you will never find yourself. You will have imprisoned yourself by your own self-doubts and limitations. *It doesn't have to be that way for you.*

Here is some food for thought: Why is it that oftentimes when we receive a compliment, even when there is ample evidence that it is true, it is hard for us to receive it and/or believe it? And yet, if someone says something negative about us, we are ready to embrace it and allow it to negatively influence our lives even when there is minimal or no evidence that it is true.

I challenge you to make a decision today to believe the good and receive it with a grateful heart. If you have made bad choices, or life has been hard for you in the past, learn from those experiences and move forward to a better life. You are worth it! There is no one who is exactly like you. Make the most of it.

Helen Keller, American author and lecturer was born with the ability to see and hear, but she contracted an illness when she was 19 months old that left her deaf and blind. Through much hard work and perseverance, she learned how to communicate. She said, "Happiness cannot come from without. It must come from within. It is not what we see and touch or that which others do for us which makes us happy; It is that which we think and feel and do, first for the other fellow and then for ourselves."

Look around and in most cases you will find people who have more hardships than you. Examine the lives of those who have chosen to be happy in spite of their hardships. What are they doing differently than you? Are their behaviors, and their choices each day different than yours? Is the way they speak to themselves different from your self-talk?

Abraham Lincoln said, "Each morning we choose to be as happy or as miserable as we want to be". What do you want for your life? Joy or misery? The choice is yours.

# *Why You Should Track Your Successes*

Keeping track of your successes will help you identify who you are, what you do well, and what you enjoy so that you can be better prepared to plan for your future.

There are several reasons to keep track of your positive accomplishments:

When you are feeling discouraged, you can review all that you have done, rejoice in your accomplishments, as well as all the obstacles you have overcome and use them as a means of self-encouragement.

Sometimes when others give us compliments, we don't always believe them. There is often a doubt in our minds about the accuracy of the compliment. But when you look back at your own positive actions and accomplishments, you can believe they are real; you did them.

Completing this exercise daily will give you an opportunity to evaluate yourself based on what you are *actually doing* rather than upon what you are *thinking or talking about doing*.

For example, when I was young, I really enjoyed dancing with my friends. Several years passed during which I did not have the opportunity to dance. As a middle-aged adult, I became free to pursue anything I wanted to explore. I remembered my dancing days with fondness, so I looked up when and where dance events were happening. I would even cut out articles so that I would remember.

I was still telling myself that I loved to dance. Surprisingly, when the opportunities came, I never went dancing. This went on for a few years. Finally, I stopped long enough to examine my behavior and realized that I had been lying to myself. Although I had fond memories of dancing, I had become a different person and really had no desire to dance. I was now having fun pursuing different interests.

Since the things you focus on are those that increase in your life, focus on and record the positive actions you take. By doing this you will find that consciously and subconsciously, you will be making better choices.

As you record your accomplishments, you may notice a trend in the behaviors that you do well, along with the ones that others appreciate in you. By evaluating the trends you see, you will be able to identify your strengths and interests. This exercise will help you to understand who you really are and this will assist you in identifying your best life and career choices.

For example, you may find that you are the happiest and most excited about life when you are interacting with other people, or when you are alone, or using your creativity, or working hard with your hands. Look for these moments and record them so that as the patterns become evident, you can look for careers which will link to your passions. When you are able to do that, you are happier and feel more accomplished in your work and in life.

By following the guidelines of usage in <u>How to Journal Your Way to Personal Success</u> and recording your findings in your journal, you will gain a clarity about who you are, what your strengths and interests are, and what personal characteristics make you special.

If you are in need of a resume for a job, school, or scholarship, the entries you have made in your journal will be a perfect outline from which you can draw the information you need and none of the relevant information will be forgotten.

Here are some quotes that may inspire you to start thinking about who you truly are:

"Learn to get in touch with the silence within yourself and know that everything in life has a purpose." – Elisabeth Kubler-Ross, Swiss American psychiatrist

"Each thought that is welcomed and recorded is a nest egg, by the side of which more will be laid." Henry David Thoreau - American author, poet, philosopher

"Most true happiness comes from one's inner life, from the disposition of the mind and soul. Admittedly, a good inner life is difficult to achieve, especially in these trying times. It takes reflection and contemplation and self-discipline." W.L. Shirer

"There are many things that will catch my eye, but there are only a few that catch my heart. It is those I consider to pursue." – Tim Redmond, journalist
Note: In your journal you will be recording and reflecting on the things that catch your heart. This will help you determine the paths to pursue to obtain fulfillment in your life.

## Instructions – Journal Productively

Keep your journal easily accessible. Keep a paper journal handy or you can use your tab or other mobile device to journal. In our companion book, My Success Journal: Writing with a Purpose (available at www.Amazon.com ), each page has a quote that was carefully chosen and intended to be a word of encouragement to you. If you would like to receive these quotes via email, please contact me at yoursuccessadvocate@gmail.com

Start looking for and thinking about the good things you can do each day. The more you look for them, the more you will find.

As an example, a friend of ours bought a new red automobile. Before he purchased his, he never noticed how many red cars were on the road. After he purchased his auto, he saw them everywhere.

Sometimes women have a similar experience when they become pregnant. Before they became pregnant, they rarely noticed any pregnant women. Once they were pregnant, it seemed as if most of the women they saw were also pregnant.

It is an amazing phenomena. Try it out for yourself. Focus on looking for something and you will start to notice it more and more each day. As you focus on looking for the good things you are doing and the obstacles that you overcome, you will happily become more aware of them each day.

Each day, take the time to review your day and make an entry of something good you have done or an obstacle your have overcome.

I think it is important to record the obstacles you have overcome because I believe that people don't give themselves enough credit for avoiding temptation or persevering to overcome obstacles. Recording these helps to build self-confidence and encourages strength in character.

If you need a motivator for the day, think about the quote of the day and ponder what it means to you.

Keep your entries simple – just the facts concerning your accomplishments or obstacles overcome.

Sample subject area entries could be:

- Positive relationship behavior
- Excellence in work – academic or employment
- Accomplishments in extra-curricular activities – hobbies, sports, academic teams, volunteering etc.
- Times when you overcame the temptation to make a wrong choice
- Times when you were kind, loving, patient, or helpful when you really didn't feel like it, but you knew it was the right thing to do.
- Times when you took responsibility for your behavior and choices – both good and bad.
- Times when you faced an obstacle and overcame it.

On a monthly basis, review your accomplishments and look for patterns or trends to help you identify strengths and interests. Create a section or chapter of your journal in which to record your strengths and interests.

Use this information to help you develop plans for the future.

Create a section or chapter in your journal in which you can record any ideas you have about your future. When you discover a career you may want to pursue, do some research about it. If possible, shadow someone who is doing the kind of work you are interested in pursuing. Talk to someone in the field, ask questions about their typical day, what they like best or least about their career, how much education is required, what the job outlook is, and what characteristics they believe a person would need to be successful in that career.

If you do not have the opportunity to talk with someone in the field which you would like to pursue, go to the library to look at the Occupational Outlook Handbook, or visit the website at www.bis.gov/oco . It is a book produced by the U.S. Bureau of Labor Statistics which gives an overview of most careers in the United States. Then check the information found in the overview against what you know about yourself and decide if this career is really a good fit for you.

When in need of a resume, review the entries in your journal concerning your accomplishments, patterns, strengths, interests and dreams for your future, and you can easily summarize the contents. This resume can be then given to potential schools, employers, or added to scholarship applications. Also, if you need a letter of recommendation from someone, give them a copy of your resume. Reading your resume will give that person the information they need to write you an excellent recommendation.

# Part 2

# Self - Discovery

# _How to Avoid the Trap of Competition_

What could be better than competition? Personal initiative. Og Mandino, author of many success oriented books, made a commentary about the difference between competition and initiative in his book <u>University of Success.</u> He said, "Initiative is everything that competition is not. Every challenge you accept, every problem you resolve, calls for person initiative. Initiative produces self-reliance with you setting your standards, whereas competing with others means that you allow <u>them</u> to set <u>your</u> goals, <u>your</u> values, and <u>your</u> rewards. Remember, competition will always place your life in the hands of others, while initiative gives you the freedom to choose your own destiny..."

The thought that competition could be a trap is foreign to most of us. If we are American, we have grown up with the idea that we must compete; that it is necessary and healthy. I would like to offer an alternative thought based on concepts gleaned from Willard and Marguerite Beecher's book <u>Beyond Success and Failure.</u>

Willard and Marguerite Beecher explain their belief that when we compete, we play by other people's rules. When we do that, we tend to give up our own ideas, creativity, personal initiative, and acceptance of personal responsibility. In contrast, they believe that we develop best by cooperating with one another rather than competing, because in competing there is always a winner and a loser.

When you are motivated by personal initiative, you can always be a winner because you set the standard. If you always strive to improve yourself and your performance, you are a winner. For example, you could be the last in a race, but if you improved on your personal speed, you have won.

By taking personal initiative when faced with a problem or situation, a person develops self-reliance. Self-reliance is a necessary component to enable a person to fulfill his potential. In becoming self-reliant, a person is able to be proactive in all experiences in life, rather than reactive to life's circumstances and situations.

When a person is competitive, he learns how to beat others involved. He has developed the skills to win in circumstances that already exist. Without self-reliance and personal initiative, although the person may exceed in accomplishments in competitive situations, they may not be able to create new and innovative solutions to problems and situations they face in life.

The competitive person looks to others to set the pace and tries to beat them, rather than pursuing his own initiatives. He then becomes dependent upon outside influences to determine his direction and level of success and ends up being reactive to life rather than proactive.

Those who are competitive also fall into the trap of always making comparisons to see who is above or below in their accomplishments. Others are our competition rather than those with whom we work in cooperation. When we cooperate with others, we are looking for the common good. When we compete, we are looking for our own good and not necessarily considering what is best for others or best in the big scheme of things.

Since the competitor is constantly comparing himself to others and determining by that yardstick the level of his success or failure, this can lead to negative thoughts and beliefs about himself that are not necessarily true. When a person is self-reliant, he does not fall into that trap. Since he does not compare himself with others, he feels no need to prove himself to them. He is free to be himself.

When one is competitive, one is always in fear of losing his position. He is constantly driven and has no time to enjoy life for life's sake. By choosing to be competitive, we have chosen to allow other's standards to become ours. Since they set the standard, we become dependent upon pursuing their praise for our efforts in life. Consequently we will do whatever is necessary to receive that praise.

One of the basic emotional attitudes of competition is hostility. We want to beat the other person; we want to be superior to him. This attitude does not allow us to fully cooperate with others for the common good. The competitive person is often a poor sport and will not engage or participate if he is not in a position to excel or win. Without winning, the competitive person has no joy. If he loses, he believes it is usually due to circumstances, or it is someone else's fault. In contrast, the self-reliant person loves to play the game for the sheer joy of playing. He loves the excitement of seeing how the game or life will turn out no matter which paths it takes. Since he does not have to prove himself, he loves to see how life's challenges can inspire new potentialities in his life.

In summary, I challenge you to consider the differences between competition and personal initiative and how they affect your life. If you feel as if you are out of balance and would like to change, use your journal activities to get more in tune with who you really are. Consider the answers to the following questions: Are you currently a very competitive person? Do you believe that you need to prove yourself to others in order to feel worthy or accomplished? Are you happy and at peace with who you are? If you are not at peace with yourself, you may want to work to develop your self-reliance and move away from the demands that comparison and competition put on your life.

# Your Thoughts Determine Your Destiny

"Watch your thoughts: They become your words.

Watch your words: They become your actions.

Watch your actions: They become your habits.

Watch your habits: They become your character.

Watch your character: It becomes your destiny."

– attributed to former Prime Minister of England, Margaret Thatcher

Notice that your destiny begins with your thoughts.

# *The Art of Pondering*
(Ponder – to think over carefully)

*Who should do it?* - Everyone

*What is it?* - Making time to stop and think. If you need to, make an appointment with yourself.

*How?* - Making and taking the time to think about the following:

About yourself
- How can you better yourself?
- How mature are you?
- Do you take responsibility for yourself?
- Do you take others' needs and well-being into consideration?
- Do you do what needs to be done when it needs to be done?
- Are you dependable?
- Do you have integrity?
- In your thoughts, on what do you focus?
- Are you keeping positive?
- Are you confusing wants and needs?
- Are your thoughts rational or are they based on negative life experiences?
- Are you progressing toward your goals, or are you just keeping busy?
- Are you accomplishing, or just participating in many activities?

About your future
- What makes you happy?
- In what areas are you successful?
- How can you use your strengths to earn a living?
- How can you use your strengths to help others?
  What would be your best career choice?

- What would you want to do with your life if you knew you could not fail?
- What characteristics would you like your future spouse to exhibit?
- What can you offer to your workplace and to your relationships?
- What is stopping you from achieving your goals?

About others
- How does your behavior affect others?
- What can you do to help someone else?
- How can you help to make someone else's life easier?
- How can you show respect, honor, and/or caring to someone?

What are your strengths and weaknesses?
- Academically
- Physically
- Socially
- Spiritually

Choosing a career that best suits you
- How do your behavior and thoughts influence the achievement of your goals?
- What are your goals?
- How will you achieve those goals?
- How will you provide for yourself after high school/college?
- Match your vision/dreams for the future with your strengths/patterns to find the most fulfilling possible career choices.
- Do your research concerning each career

_Where?_ – Anywhere you find yourself with a few free moments or make a designated quiet place to ponder.

_Why is it important?_ - Pondering is important because it is our one chance to connect with our true selves.

# *Goal Setting*

At the beginning of any trip you want to take, you must have a plan. If you are going to the grocery store, you must know where it is and how you will get there. You may want to make a list of the groceries you would like to get so that you can fulfill your purpose in going there.

If you are going on a vacation, your time is limited. The best way to get the most for the money spent is to have a plan. Determining the sites you would like to see, the activities in which you want to participate, how much money and time is available to do everything you want to do will give you the necessary information you need to get the most out of your vacation.

The same is true in life. As on a vacation, we have a limited time here on earth. If we want to live a fulfilling life, we should have a plan. If we don't have a plan, time will pass us by, and we will get to the end of our lives only to realize that we had lived in reaction to life rather than living in a proactive way to live the life we wanted. Fortunately, it doesn't have to be that way for you. You don't have to come to the end of your life with unfulfilled dreams. No matter what your age or circumstance, you can start today to make a plan.

Another way of saying "make a plan" is to describe it as "set a goal". I am sure that you have heard of goal setting. Perhaps you are not sure where to start. It is a lot easier than you may think.

There are only five components to setting goals.

A. Determine what the goal will be. It must be realistic and measureable.
B. Write it down.
C. What steps need to be taken to acomplish the goal?
D. Create a timeline during which the goal will be accomplished.
E. When the goal has been achieved what will it look like?

How do you determine what your life goals will be?

Start thinking about who you are, identifying your strengths and weaknesses, your interests, and your abilities. What would you like to do if you could do anything? Believe in yourself. Think positively.

Many books have been written about the phenomenom of positive thinking. Normal Vincent Peale, internationally known American author and speaker wrote volumes on the effectiveness of positive thinking and supported his teaching with thousands of stories of tragedy turned to success. James Allen wrote a book entitled, "As A Man Thinketh". In this book he talks about how our thoughts influence who we become. For example, if you think of yourself as a leader you can become one. If you think of yourself as being incapable of succeeding, you will probably not succeed. Henry Ford, American industrialist and founder of the Ford Motor Company, supported this concept in his quote. "If you think you can do a thing or you think you can't, you are right.". If you doubt the effectiveness of positive thinking for yourself, do an experiment.

For a day or more, speak and allow yourself to be exposed to only positive things via conversations, TV, computer, social media, and reading. See how you feel and examine your accomplishments during this period of time. Do the same for the negative and compare the results. I am sure you will find that thinking postively produces more positive results in your life as well as a feeling of peace and well-being within yourself.

As you start to take control of your thoughts, it is crucial to replace negative thoughts and patterns of behavior with something positive. When you try to eliminate a negative thought or pattern, a void will be created. If you do not fill this void with positive thoughts and behaviors, you will return to your original negative thoughts and behaviors. When you attempt to make a change for the better, it will feel uncomfortable. You must persevere through the discomfort until the new positive thoughts and behaviors feel comfortable to you. At that moment you will be changed and will have no desire to return to any negativity in your life. We gain confidence to advance and pride in ourselves when we find that we are able to overcome obstacles and persevere through difficulties.

When you create a goal, it must be realistic and measureable. For example, if my goal is to be a professional race car driver at the Daytona Speedway where the cars travel at approximately 200 m.p.h., but my physical reaction time is slow, it would not be realistic to set a goal to become a professional race car driver.

My physical inability to react quickly enough to track conditions and other cars would prohibit my success. If I loved the sport of auto racing, I could set a goal to do something associated with it, such as announcer, pit crew, mechanic, ticket taker, race coordinator, or seller of promotional materials. The goal must also be measurable. An effective goal statement would not be, "I will do something associated with auto racing." An effective goal statement could be, "Within the next five years, I will become a pit crew member for a race car driver." The goal must be specific and measurable so that you can know exactly what you are working toward and when you will have achieved it.

<u>Write it down.</u>

Why is it so important to write down your goals? In a study done at the Dominican University by Gail Matthews, those who had written goals accomplished much more than those who just thought about their goals but did not write them down. (http://www.dominican.edu/dominicannews/stud y-backs-up-strategies-for-achieving-goals). When goals are written down, it is the first step in making them real. When you are able to write a goal down, it means that your have thought about it enough that it has become a solid thought in your mind. You can visualize it happening. It is at this point that it begins to happen. When a goal is written, you can look back on it and see concretely what you want to do.

You can experiment with this yourself. Make a goal for yourself in your mind, but do not write it down. Make another goal and write it down. In two months, look back and see which goal you are closer to accomplishing or which you have already accomplished.

## What steps need to be taken to accomplish the goal?

It is important to think this through to determine what steps need to be taken and to write them down. There may be many steps to accomplishing each goal. If you don't write them down, the steps you need to take may become muddled in your mind and hinder you from accomplishing the goal. If you begin to write down the steps needed and it seems overwhelming, break the goal down into smaller goals. It is so important to just get started.

For example, if your goal is to lose weight and the number of steps needed to accomplish this seems too impossible for you, begin in a small way. Begin a journal and write down everything you eat each day for a week. If you can do more than that, make journal entries about how you feel when you eat, such as hungry, lonely, angry, frustrated, happy. You may enter what the occasion was for eating, such as mealtime, birthday party etc. Look back on those entries to make an honest evaluation of what you are really eating and why. You can then use that information to help you determine the steps you need to take to begin your journey of losing weight.

Here is an example of some steps that could be taken to help someone lose weight:

- Establish what I am currently eating
- Establish if I am eating in reaction to feelings or circumstances rather than because I am hungry.
- Eat a moderate or small portion of healthy breakfast each morning.
- Snack on small helpings of protein between meals.

- Eat a balanced diet complete with fruits and vegetables in moderate or small portions for lunch and dinner.
- Drink more water.
- Avoid sugar and high calorie drinks.
- Begin an exercise regimen doing something that is fun for me. More specifically, this statement could be, I will walk at a moderate to vigorous speed for 15 min. each day.

## Create a timeline during which you will accomplish the goals.

It is important to set a timeline. If you don't create a timeline you will not feel accountable to yourself or anyone else to complete the goal. It is similar to getting a homework or job assignment; if there is no deadline, it rarely gets finished because people get preoccupied with the busyness of life.

Some examples of timelines for short term goals, using the above mentioned goal could be:

- For 1 week, I will record my intake of food, starting today.
- For 1 week, I will record the occasions of my eating and how I felt about it, starting today.
- My new eating program will start 1 week from today.

Some examples of timelines for a long term goal could be:

- In one year I will have lost 35 pounds
- In one year I will be exercising for at least 30 minutes 3 times per week.

## What will the goal look like when it is achieved?

It is important to visualize what the accomplishment of your goal will look like for two reasons. By visualizing the accomplishment you will help it come to pass. (Remember the power of positive thinking?). Secondly, by writing down what it looks like, you will know when you have completed the goal.

Some examples of this using the weight loss goal could look like this:

- At the end of one month I will weigh 5 pounds less.
- At the end of one month I will reevaluate my progress and rewrite and adjust further goals as necessary.

By utilizing these five steps to goal setting, you are well on your way to accomplishing your dreams. Now that you know how to set goals, you may want to create some long term goals also, such as: by the end of the year I will have accomplished _____. In five years I will_____. In ten years_____ etc.

It is important to review your progress toward your goals on a consistent basis. By doing so, you will keep honest with yourself and keep yourself on track to complete what you have started.

# Part 3

# Thoughts and Challenges

# POSITIVE ATTITUDE

What is positive attitude? It is maintaining peace and hope in the midst of trials. It is a habit of looking for solutions rather than focusing on problems. It is the ability to control your thoughts and attitudes in a way that you are not overcome by adversity.

## CHALLENGE:

Look for the good in others and in situations. Think and speak only things that are positive. If you find yourself thinking a negative thought or saying negative words, stop and make a change.

Think about what you allow into your life. Choose to:
- Watch (TV, movies, computer, etc.),
- Listen (radio, CDs, other people talking etc.) and participate in *only positive things* and see how your life changes for the better

Be a role model of a person with a positive attitude.

# *RESPONSIBILITY*

What is being responsible? Seeing what needs to be done and doing it without anyone asking. Taking credit for the good things you accomplish, acknowledging the mistakes you make, and as much as possible, making right what you have done wrong. In essence, being responsible is being answerable for your behavior. It is being dependable and trustworthy. Being responsible is doing the right thing, even when it is not comfortable or easy.

## *CHALLENGE*:

Take time to reflect on the degree to which you accept personal responsibility.

- Are you making a plan for your life after high
- school/college/career change? Are you taking advantage of the resources available to you?
- Are you living a life which exemplifies responsibility as described above? How can you do better? Are you working to be the best you can be?

Take action on the results of the above reflection.

- Reflect and act on how you can be a more responsible citizen – in class, at work, at home, in your community. What actions can you take to make your world a better place now than when you entered it?

The following article is a tremendous tool to help us look at many aspects of maturity. By reviewing these traits of a mature person, we can determine how mature we are and in which areas we have yet to grow and develop.

## MATURITY – ARE WE THERE YET?
By Ann Landers, columnist

Maturity is many things
- It is the ability to base a judgment on the big picture, the long haul.
- It means being able to resist the urge for immediate gratification and opt for the course of action that will pay off later. One of the characteristics of the youth is, "I want it now". Grown-up people can wait.
- Maturity is perseverance – the ability to sweat out a project or a situation in spite of heavy opposition and discouraging setbacks, and stick with it until it is finished. The adult who is constantly changing jobs, changing friends and changing mates is immature. He/she cannot stick it out because he/she has not grown up.
- Maturity is the ability to control anger and settle differences without violence or destruction.
- The mature person can face unpleasantness, frustrations, discomfort and defeat without collapsing or complaining. He/she knows he/she can't have everything his/her own way every time. He/she is able   to defer to circumstances, to other people – and to time. He/she knows when to compromise and is not too proud to do it.

- Maturity is humility. It is being big enough to say, "I was wrong." And when he/she is right, the mature person need not experience the satisfaction of saying, "I told you so."
- Maturity is the ability to live up to your responsibilities, and this means being dependable. It means keeping your word. Dependability is the hallmark of integrity. Do you mean what you say – and do you say what you mean? Unfortunately, the world is filled with people who can't be counted on. When you need them most, they are among the missing. They never seem to come through in the clutches. They break promises and substitute alibis for performance. They show up late or not at all. They are confused and disorganized. Their lives are a chaotic maze of broken promises, former friends, unfinished business and good intentions that somehow never materialize. They are always a day late and a dollar short.
- Maturity is the ability to make a decision and stand by it. Immature people spend their lives exploring endless possibilities and then do nothing. Action requires courage. Without courage, little is accomplished.
- Maturity is the ability to harness your abilities and your energies and do more than is expected. The mature person refuses to settle for mediocrity. He/she would rather aim high and miss the mark than aim low – and make it.
- Maturity is the art of living in peace with that which we cannot change, the courage to

change that which should be changed, no matter what it takes, and the wisdom to know the difference.

# COURAGE

Think about the courage that was shown by the pilgrims, our founding fathers, and our ancestors when they left everything they knew and came to an unknown place to start a new and hopefully better life. Think about the courage shown by our Armed Forces to keep us free. Think about the courage it takes you, your friends and family to make the right choices and do the right things even when it is not comfortable and/or easy.

Courage can be defined as, the state or quality of mind or spirit that enables one to face danger with self-possession, confidence, and resolution; bravery; valor. Courage suggests a reserve of moral strength on which one may draw in time of emergency.

# CHALLENGE:

With your family and friends, talk about the daily challenges each of you faces that call on you to be courageous (see definitions above)

Stand up for at least one thing that is good and right and true each day. At the end of the day, look yourself in the mirror and be proud that you were courageous that day.

Be courageous enough to find (which means make a plan to develop yourself) and be your best self.

# COMMUNICATION/RESPECT

When families and friends get together, communication is essential. When we learn to communicate properly, we are able to express our thoughts, needs, and expectations as well as listen to the thoughts, needs, and expectations of those around us. Consequently, we can learn to live in peace with each other.

Definitions:
Positive communication is reflected through praise, sincere compliments, encouragement, expressions of gratitude, truth/honesty, belief/trust, sympathy, humor/laughing with, advice/instruction, sharing of good news, greetings, support.

Negative communication is manifested via put-downs, swearing, biting sarcasm, name-calling, laughing at, complaining, having an air of expectancy – people owe you whatever you want, gossip/rumor, yelling, insincere flattery, racial and sexual insults, lying/manipulating, blaming.

# CHALLENGE:

If there is someone with whom you are holding a grudge, make a decision to forgive that person. Look for the good in that person and/or think about that person from a more positive perspective.

Open the doors of communication by talking with that person in a non-emotional manner. Listen to what the other person has to say and try to understand situations from his/her perspective.

Then, in a calm manner, express your thoughts, feelings, needs or expectations.

If you are already at peace with everyone, congratulations! As you get together with friends or family, remember and share with each other the happy times you spent together. Also, you can create new memories by talking and doing positive things together.

If the people with whom you spend time have different expectations about how holidays or other get-togethers should be celebrated or experienced, talk about what each person is expecting and be willing to compromise so that everyone's needs and expectations are met to some degree.

Allow others the right to have their own opinions, even if those opinions do not agree with yours. Doing this will have a dramatic effect on improving your relationships.

*Starting communication:*

Example questions to ask in considering this concept could be:

- What does being able to communicate in a positive manner mean to me?
- How do I see this exhibited in school, at work, in life, at home? Give examples.
- How would someone know that I was a person who could communicate in a positive manner?
- What behaviors would they see?
- Do you know a person whom you consider to have good communication skills?
    - What are your thoughts about that person?

- Do you know a person whom you consider to have poor communication skills?
  - What are your thoughts about that person?
- What are the consequences of being able to communicate in a positive manner?

- What are some consequences of being able to communicate in a negative manner?
- How would being able to communicate positively or negatively help or hinder me from having what I want in life?
- On a scale of one to ten, how often am I able to communicate in a positive manner? 1 being never and 10 being always.
- Using that same scale, how much more do I want to communicate in a positive manner by the end of this year?
- What must I do differently to achieve that goal?
- Am I willing to do it?

# SELF-CONCEPT/SELF-RESPECT

Take a moment to reflect. How do I see myself? Is this view accurate? What are my strengths and weaknesses? By knowing them, I can maximize and appreciate my strengths and overcome or minimize my weaknesses.

The definition of concept can be a general idea or understanding, especially one derived from specific instances or occurrences.

Self can be defined as, the qualities of one person distinguishing him from another; personality or character; individuality or an individual's consciousness of his own being or identity.

Definitions of respect are to honor, feel or show esteem for, and willingness to show appreciation for.

## CHALLENGE:

Take 15 minutes per day to think about yourself – strengths, weaknesses, how you are perceived by others and by yourself, and ask yourself if the views are accurate.

After taking a few days working on the first challenge, write down your thoughts.

Reflect on what you have written and decide what you would like to keep the same about yourself and what you would like to change.

What could you do to improve yourself by the end of this year if there were no obstacles in your way? Write down your ideas.

Write down one thing you could do differently this month to move you toward this change. Each month, reevaluate your progress and add one thing you could do differently to take you closer to your goals.

# _LOVE/FRIENDSHIP_

A friend can be defined as a person whom one knows, likes and trusts. From my personal experience, I would include, "a person who wants what is best for you".

Love can be defined as an intense affectionate concern for another person. Unfortunately, most of us define love based on our experiences, whether good or bad. If our experiences were not truly loving, the result is that we have a distorted view of what love is, and this often leads to despair and heartache.

In 1 Corinthians 13:4-8, God gives the definitive description of love.

> Love is patient, love is kind, and is not jealous; love does not brag and is not arrogant, does not act unbecomingly; it does not seek its own, is not provoked, does not take into account a wrong suffered, does not rejoice in unrighteousness, but rejoices in the truth; bears all things, believes all things, hopes all things, endures all things. Love never fails.
> (The Open Bible edition, New American Standard Bible p. 1108, Thomas Nelson Pub. 1977)

"When one has learned how to love, one has learned how to live." Robert Lechner, professor, author

# *CHALLENGE*:

Make a list of the qualities you include when defining friendship. Which qualities do you include when defining love? Write them down.

Write down the names of all those you love and who love you. Do they/you possess the qualities you listed above? If not, what additional qualities do they possess that enable you to feel loved by them? What additional qualities do you express to show love to others?

Repeat the exercise described in #2 including the names of those you consider friends.

After thinking about the qualities you and your friends/those you love bring to a relationship, if the qualities you listed are missing, this would be a good opportunity to start conversations relating to ways you and they can improve your relationships.

Look at your behaviors objectively, as if a camera were taking a movie of your actions, to see if you are acting loving to others.

Are you patient with people? Even the most annoying and inconsiderate ones?

Are you kind to everyone you meet, including those closest to you? Sometimes we are kinder and more polite to strangers than we are to those closest to us.

Do you envy others of their successes or happiness?

Do you find yourself boasting about your accomplishments?

Are you so proud that you cannot have compassion toward others?

Are you rude, and then make excuses about why it is acceptable?

Are you always looking out for yourself, without ever considering the impact your actions, words, or inactions will have on others?

Do you get angry easily?

Do you hold a grudge?

Do you enjoy gossiping and sharing the weaknesses or failings of others?

Are you excited for others when they achieve their goals and desires?

Do you try to help others and look out for their best interests?

Do you trust people?

Do you have hope for the future?

Do you continue in your efforts for good even when obstacles arise?

My ultimate challenge to you is this: Try to act loving as evidenced by the 5$^{th}$ challenge, which asks you to look at your behaviors objectively and answer the questions which follow that challenge in a positive way. If you do, you will find that it will transform your life for the better.

# COMMITMENT /PERSEVERANCE

Commitment is a promise to do what you said you would do.

Perseverance is continuing to work toward a goal even when it is difficult and the obstacles seem insurmountable. Never give up on your passions.

## CHALLENGE:

Evaluate your behaviors
-   Do you keep your commitments?
-   Do you put forth the extra effort necessary to go from mediocre/average to excellent?
-   Do you keep on trying when things get hard or do you give up?
-   For your own awareness, list instances in which you kept your commitments and worked past the difficulties.
-   For your own awareness, list instances in which you did not keep your commitments or times when you gave up when the going got tough.
-   If you find areas that need improvement, what can you do differently in the future to make the necessary changes?

# HONESTY/HONOR

To be honest is, not lying, cheating, stealing or taking unfair advantage; honorable, truthful, trustworthy; having or manifested integrity or truth; genuine; sincere.

Words used to describe honor are: respect, esteem, reverence, good reputation, glory, fame, distinction, a title conferred for achievement, and personal integrity, maintained without legal or other obligations. To be a person of honor to ourselves, to our family, and to our country is a tall order, but if you choose to, you will rise to the occasion.

# CHALLENGE:

Each day we make choices. As you make your choices, ask yourself if you are being honest – to yourself and to others.

Is what you are saying or doing really honest or is it merely convenient?

Do a personal inventory. Reflect on your life. Are you a person of honor?

Do you value others, respect their feelings, and give them the freedom to have their own opinions?

Do you strive to protect yourself from destructive decisions and/or actions?

If you are not living up to the standard you would like to develop for yourself, what changes need to be made? How and when can you make them?

# *INTEGRITY*

A person of integrity is characterized by a rigid adherence to a code of behavior;

**I**nterested in the well-being of others

**N**ice, kind, generous

**T**rustworthy, warranting trust

**E**steem – to be well thought of, to have a good reputation

**G**enuine – not characterized by deception or fraud

**R**espectable – of or appropriate to good or proper behavior; having an acceptable appearance

**I**nternalize the qualities of positive attitude, responsibility, courage, positive communication, self-respect, respect for others, love, commitment, and honesty

**T**ruthful – to be honest, a person of your word

**Y**earning to make the most of myself while helping others do the same.

In my opinion, integrity is the internalization and application of all the above mentioned character traits.

# CHALLENGE:

In every area of your life, encourage yourself to live a life of integrity.

# Part 4

# Appendix

# _Acknowledgements_

I want to thank God for always being there for me - to love me, protect me, help, guide and teach me, even before I realized He was there. I thank you God for Your faithfulness and everlasting love. Thank you for helping me with all that I do.

I want to thank my husband, John, for being the wind beneath my wings. You are my greatest cheerleader. You love me more than I could ever imagine being loved. I appreciate your wisdom, guidance, encouragement and support in all God asks me to do. I appreciate your honesty in reviewing all that I propose to do. Without your input and encouragement, this book as well as many other good things I have done, would not have been accomplished.

Thank you to all my family and friends who encouraged me in my efforts and helped me with their suggestions and ideas.

## *About the Author*

Frances Marx is originally from Chicago, Ill. and has lived in Sarasota since 1985. To her, each day living in Sarasota is like one more day in paradise. In her spare time, she loves to ride her bike and play Pickleball with her husband.

Frances is happily married. She is a well - respected certified counselor, educator, author, speaker, entrepreneur, and family oriented woman. Frances is highly creative and once problems are identified, she thrives on finding unique solutions.

She is also zealous about helping others find their true calling in life consequently Frances becomes a success advocate for everyone she meets. It each stage of her life, Frances has loved her work and desires others to have the same opportunity.

Through her life experiences, Frances has uncovered some basic truths that she believes, if applied, will help those who use How to Journal Your Way to Personal Success to discover, value, and learn to appreciate the gifts they have within. They can then use that information to continue on their journey toward self-fulfillment and positive contribution to others' lives.

I hope that my achievements in life will be these:

    That I have left the world a better place for my being here

    That I have taught my children faith in God, courage, perseverance and strength

    That I have made a positive difference in the lives of all those I have met

    That I have been able to reflect God's love to others as He has loved me

Frances Marx

Thank your for your interest

I would love to hear from you! I am very interested in receiving your input concerning the ways in which <u>How to Journal Your Way to Personal Success</u> has impacted your life.

For booking speaking engagements, information concerning seminars and webinars, or to order more products, contact:

Frances Marx
Your Success Advocate
Speaker, Author, Mentor

Email: yoursuccessadvocate@gmail.com

Other publications by Frances Marx:

<u>My Success Journal: Writing With a Purpose</u>

<u>Mall Order Bride: A True Cinderella Story</u>

<u>My Success Journal: A Guided Tour on the Journey to Self-Discovery</u>

Made in the USA
San Bernardino, CA
19 May 2014